Survival Guide
for Parents

How to Avoid Screwing Up Your Kids
Or Losing Your Own Sanity

Survival Guide for Parents

How to Avoid Screwing Up Your Kids Or Losing Your Own Sanity

Mickey Michaels, B.A., M.A., M.B.A

Illustrations by Richard Foss

Possibility Press
6608 East Hill Dr.
Austin, TX 78731

ISBN 0-9644761-1-8

LCCN 94-74608

First printing 1995

Attention: Organizations, Corporations, and Educational Institutions: Quantity discounts are available on bulk purchases of this book for educational purposes, gifts, or fund raising. Special books or book excerpts can also be created to fit specific needs. For information, please contact our Special Sales Department, 6608 East Hill Dr., Austin, TX 78731, 512-418-0067.

About This Book

Yes, it is possible to be a good parent, an effective parent, and even enjoy the process! The author shares her experiences in a series of simple but profound observations. Many of them are humorous. All of them will make you think. As the author says,

"Kids will do the strangest things.
Don't take it personally. Don't think you have failed.
Keep your perspective and, above all, keep your sense of humor!"

About the Author

Mickey Michaels has been a parent for 20 years, a single parent for 13 of these. She has a Bachelor's and Master's degree in psychology and a Master's degree in business. She has managed to combine parenting with a full-time career and a full personal life—and to enjoy all three pursuits.

Mickey has experienced all of the following "life cycle" stages: Single, career woman. Married, working wife. Stay-at-home wife and mother. Working mother. Divorced, working single parent.

She has survived the day-care days, the "latch-key kid", the bizarre behavior of adolescence, and the dreaded teenage years.

She has raised a daughter who is independent, self-sufficient, capable, polite, hard-working, and well-adjusted. If this is hard to believe, what is even more surprising is that she and her daughter truly like, respect, and enjoy each other.

Introduction

I would love to be able to say that as a parent, I knew exactly what I was doing every step along the way. Unfortunately, I can't say that.

The fact is I was terrified! I knew just enough psychology to know that parents can really screw up their kids. And I was afraid I would do just that.

When we brought Patti home from the hospital and I looked down at this tiny, helpless infant who was totally dependent on me, my strongest feeling was panic:

> *"These things ought to come with instructions!!"*

Our kids will survive, no matter what mistakes we make. But over the years, I have learned some things we can do as parents to make life a lot more pleasant in the short run and to benefit our kids in the long run.

If you're happy and comfortable with whatever you're already doing, keep on doing it! But if you're not totally satisfied with the results you're getting, try something else. This book can give you some ideas for other approaches to try. Maybe they will work better for you.

And it might prepare you in advance for some situations you haven't yet faced but will in the future.

So here they are, the things I've learned that I wish someone had handed me as I was bringing my baby home from the hospital:

SURVIVAL GUIDE FOR PARENTS
How to Avoid Screwing Up Your Kids
Or Losing Your Own Sanity

(So as not to slight either gender, I have alternated the pronouns he/she and him/her throughout the book.)

Table of Contents

Your First Fears

♦ When your baby cries, it doesn't mean you've done something wrong.

♦ You can't spoil a baby by picking him up too much.

♦ You can't spoil a baby by letting her cry occasionally either.

- Don't put your baby on a schedule you can't live with.

- Babies are more adaptable than you are.

♦ Babies can fall asleep anywhere—
   unless you teach them that they
   require absolute quiet.

♦ Your baby won't sleep through the
   night until you are willing to let him.

- "Bonding" with your baby comes from doing the dirty work.

- Babies understand much more than you think they do.

- Babies can sense when you are tired, upset, or tense. You need your sleep as much as the baby does.

Your Next Fears

♦ Leaving your baby with a sitter is much more difficult for you than it is for the baby.

♦ Many sitters have more experience with babies than you do.

♦ Leave a phone number where you can be reached if there is a problem.

♦ If the sitter does not call you, that means there are no problems.

♦ If you call home to check, you will probably wake the baby.

♦ A breast-feeding baby will drink a bottle of formula if she is hungry.

♦ An occasional bottle of formula will not spoil your baby.

♦ Get out of the house and away from the baby at least once a week. It will make you a better parent.

Separation Anxiety

Separation Anxiety

♦ This is a phenomenon experienced primarily by parents.

♦ Children will scream bloody murder when you leave them but will stop as soon as you are out of sight.

♦ Resist the temptation to go back and check on them.

19

- Independence is a learned skill.

- Children can't learn to be away from you unless you let them.

- Your child does not yearn for you every moment you are out of his sight.

- Don't let this hurt your feelings. It's a good sign.

Dangers of the Toddler Years

♦ Don't leave anything dangerous where a child can reach it.

♦ Don't leave anything irreplaceable where a child can reach it.

♦ Children can reach much more than you think they can.

♦ If you repeat the names of objects and actions, your child will learn to speak at an early age.

♦ Your child will learn to speak eventually, no matter what you do.

♦ A child who speaks is much more pleasant to interact with than one who doesn't.

♦ Behavior that is rewarded will be repeated.

♦ Behavior that is not rewarded will not be repeated.

♦   A child considers negative attention more rewarding than no attention at all.

♦   If you ignore a child when he is playing quietly but fuss at him when he gets into trouble, which behavior do you think will be repeated?

Everything you do
sends a message
to your child,
whether you mean to or not.

———

- If a child gets what she wants by whining or crying, what will she learn from this?

- If a child gets what he wants by saying appropriate words, what will he learn from this?

♦   Enjoy dressing your little ones the way you want to. By the time they get to be 3 or 4 years old, they will have their own very definite ideas.

♦   If a child does not like something in the store, you can be sure she will never wear it.

♦   If a child does like something in the store, there is still a good chance she may never wear it.

♦ How a child feels about the way he looks is more important than the money you spent on the outfit.

♦ The older the child gets, the more her taste will differ from yours.

♦ A parent's taste in clothes is hopelessly outdated.

Single Parents

♦ The greatest thing about being a single parent is that there's nobody else around to screw it up.

♦ The hardest thing about being a single parent is trying to do everything yourself.

♦ You can't do everything alone.

♦ Don't let this make you feel inadequate. No one can make it through life alone. Only fools try.

- If you're trying to keep a perfect house, lower your standards.

- If you're trying to be Ward or June Cleaver, forget it.

- Ward and June Cleaver never had to deal with the issues you do.

Preserving Your Own Mental Health

Preserving Your Own Mental Health

♦ Teach kids early on that certain times are "grown-up times" when kids need to entertain themselves. This may save your sanity.

♦ Consider using the *"Blood and Bones Rule"*:
  During "grown-up times," kids are not to disturb you unless blood or broken bones are involved.

♦   If you give in when your child interrupts your adult time, he will do it again and again.

♦   Don't allow yourself to be manipulated by guilt. You don't owe your child every moment of your time.

♦   A mentally healthy adult with a balanced life makes a better parent than a frustrated, frazzled, overwhelmed parent.

- If you push yourself beyond your limits in trying to do things for your child, you will find yourself feeling pressured, frustrated, and angry at the child.

- This is not fair to yourself or the child.

♦   It's a child's job to ask for everything.
     It's a parent's job to set limits.

♦   An unhappy martyr does not make a
     good parent.

Building Your Child's Character

♦ Your child is a blank slate. Everything you are and everything you do makes an indelible impression.

♦ Children learn far more from our example than from anything we tell them.

You can't ask more of your child than you ask of yourself.

- ◆ If we want our children to learn kindness, we must treat them kindly.

- ◆ If we want them to show respect, we must treat them with respect.

♦ If we want our children to learn responsibility, we must be responsible.

♦ If we want them to learn integrity, we must keep our word.

♦ Children are constantly observing who we are, how we act, and the results we get. They draw their own conclusions from that.

♦ "Do as I say, not as I do" is doomed to failure. As Emerson said:

*Who you are speaks so loudly,
I can't hear what you say.*

Am I Doing the Right Thing?

♦ In parenting, there is only one absolute truth. That is:

> *"There is no absolute truth."*

♦ Everything you do will have its pros and cons.

43

♦ Don't expect that you should be able to find "the perfect answer."

♦ There is no perfect answer, but some outcomes are better than others.

♦ The best way to judge how you're doing is simply to look at the results.

◆ Do you *like* the person your child is becoming? *(This is different from <u>love</u>.)*

◆ Is your child a person you (and others) enjoy being around?

◆ Will his present behavior and attitudes serve him well as an adult?

♦ If you're not comfortable with the results you're getting, try another method.

♦ Don't be afraid of losing your child's respect if you admit that something is not working.

♦ Willingness to own up to a bad choice and correct it is a behavior your child would do well to learn.

♦ Think about the effect on your child before you act or speak.

♦ Words said in haste can do incalculable harm.

♦ Practicing this will teach you patience you never had before. It will make you a better person.

The Struggle for Control

♦ It costs you nothing to let your child make certain choices for himself.

♦ Choices give children a sense of competence and control.

♦ Children who are given some control feel less need to rebel.

♦ It is much easier for your child to accept and to do a task if you give her some control over when it is to be done.

♦ If you set a reasonable deadline but let her choose the exact timing, she still feels she has some control.

♦ The more control you give her, the less she will resist you.

♦ If a child has had no experience making decisions along the way, how can she suddenly become a good decision-maker when she leaves home?

♦ Good decision-making is a skill your child must learn.

♦ Structuring choices for your child is a skill you must learn.

♦ When you structure a choice for a child, both options must be acceptable to you.

♦ It defeats the purpose if you impose your preferences on him.

♦ Well-structured choices teach a child that life involves trade-offs.

♦ Well-structured choices allow a child to see that consequences (good or bad) follow as a logical result of her own behavior.

♦ This type of structure teaches a child to accept responsibility for her own actions.

♦ Allowing your child to make his own choices will enhance your relationship.

♦ When he accepts responsibility for his own outcomes, he does not see you as a "bad guy" who is making his life unpleasant.

♦ Set certain limits, then let your child choose within that framework.

♦ Think through your decisions. Have a reason for whatever rules or limits you set.

- When your child asks you for a reason, this is not a sign of disrespect.

- It does not diminish your authority or your child's respect for you to explain your reasons.

♦ "Do it because I say so" causes a child to resent your authority.

♦ Constantly telling children what to do has only two outcomes, both of which are bad:

1. They ignore or disobey us.

2. They obey but resent it and don't learn from it.

♦ If a child makes a bad choice and has to live with the consequences, she will fully learn why that was a bad choice.

♦ Let children make their own mistakes and learn from them, as long as the consequences are not fatal.

Self-esteem

♦ Kids live up to—or down to—our expectations of them.

♦ Kids are much more capable than we think they are.

♦ Self-esteem is one of the greatest gifts you can give your child.

♦ Everything you do or say to him either builds it up or tears it down.

- Praise—for even the smallest things—builds self-esteem.

- Criticism—no matter how well-meaning—tears it down.

♦ You are a mirror through which your child sees herself.

♦ Children find it hard to believe in themselves, so you must make your support believable.

♦ Catch your child doing something right.

♦ Be specific about what you admire and appreciate in his behavior.

♦ Praise your child for behavior that will serve her well as an adult.

♦ Do not take good behavior for granted.

♦ If you want the behavior to be repeated, you must give positive reinforcement.

♦ If your child wants to talk to you, your response sends him a message.

♦ Much of the day-to-day trivia that a young child wants to share will be totally boring to an adult. You must never let her know this.

♦ If you show no interest in the little things early on, she will not come to you later with the big things you do want to hear.

♦ Unconditional love does not mean you have no standards.

♦ Sometimes it's necessary to correct a child's behavior.

♦ You will love your child no matter what, but some behavior is unacceptable.

You must make the distinction
between
disapproval of the behavior
and
disapproval of the child!!

♦ It's destructive to belittle a child. What he learns from this is, *"I'm not good enough."*

♦ What you want him to learn is that certain behaviors produce certain results.

♦ Address the behavior, not the child's character.

♦ *"When you do this...(whatever the action is)..., it hurts other people's feelings/makes it unpleasant for other people to be around you/etc."*

♦ Your child learns something every time you react to her behavior.

♦ Remember what it is you want her to learn:

> *"Good behavior will produce good results."*

Chores and Responsibility

- Children who take on responsibility have higher self-esteem than those who don't.

- A child who contributes something to the family feels like part of a team.

- A child who contributes nothing does not value himself or feel valued.

♦ A parent can structure responsibility to be a great learning experience for the child.

♦ Something valuable will be learned if the consequences of doing or not doing the task fall on the child, not on you.

♦ If the task gets done, she gets a certain benefit. If the task is not done, she does not get the benefit.

- Allow your child to experience the natural consequences of his own behavior.

- What he will learn from this is that there are benefits from assuming responsibility and bad consequences from letting it slide.

◆ Don't assign your child a chore that will drive you crazy if it goes undone.

◆ You won't be able to resist nagging.

◆ What the child will learn from this is that you are a nag.

♦ You can easily teach a child that, within a family, it's everyone's responsibility to pick up after himself.

♦ The way you do this is by setting the example.

♦ You can't expect a child to pick up her things when your own are lying around.

♦ An easy way to enlist cooperation and avoid resentment is to make household tasks a joint effort.

♦ If a child sees you working and pitches in to help, he feels like part of a team.

♦ If you tell him to work while you sit on the couch reading, he feels like a slave.

♦ The words you use when you ask your child to do something can be crucial.

♦ *"I need"* makes her feel like she is supporting you.

♦ *"You have to"* makes her feel like you are controlling her.

♦ Recognizing that something needs to be done requires a greater level of maturity than actually doing the task.

♦ Your child may learn to do both by the time he owns his own home.

Your Room is a Disaster

Your Room Is a Disaster

♦ It will be a constant source of conflict and frustration if you insist that a child keep her own room perfectly neat and clean at all times.

♦ A child will not find it an unreasonable burden to keep the family living areas clean if he has his own space that he can control.

◆ It's a matter of consideration for others that everyone picks up his own clutter from the common areas.

◆ This does not apply to the child's own room.

◆ You don't have to live there. If you keep the door shut, you don't even have to look at it.

♦ The older your child gets, the more the ability to control his own space becomes a central need for him.

♦ If you don't turn it into a control issue, eventually your child will decide to clean up her own room.

♦ If you make it a power struggle, she will resist you no matter what.

♦ If you're not on his back constantly, a child can accept that there are times when you simply can't stand the clutter in his room any longer.

♦ Fear of insects, rodents, or disease sometimes works as a reason to do something about cleaning the room.

Money and Responsibility

♦ Don't feel guilty if you can't afford to buy your child many of the luxuries she wants.

♦ All too often, the adults who are least satisfied throughout life are those who have been given the most luxuries as children.

You do your child no service
if you deny him
the sense of accomplishment
and self-esteem
that comes from
earning something desirable
through his own efforts.

♦ One of the greatest gifts you can give your child is the opportunity to earn money, to manage it, and to decide how to spend it.

♦ This, more than anything else, can teach her that the rewards she can expect from life will depend on what she contributes to it.

♦ It's a parent's obligation to provide a child with the necessities of life. The luxuries are optional.

♦ It's very difficult for a child to distinguish between necessities and luxuries.

♦   Shoes are a necessity. Designer tennis shoes are a luxury.

♦   Stereos, TVs, VCRs, and CDs are luxuries.

♦   A car of one's own when a person turns 16 is a luxury.

♦   You can avoid a lot of conflict, teach your child a valuable lesson, and build confidence and self-esteem if you will adopt and state the following policy:

> *"I will buy you the things you actually need. If you want more things than I am able or willing to buy for you, you can earn the money to buy them for yourself."*

♦   You can buy some benefits for yourself while teaching your child responsibility if you pay him for doing certain chores around the house.

♦   If the child does them, he gets paid. If not, he doesn't.

♦   He learns the natural consequences of his own behavior:

Effort = reward.   No effort = no reward.

♦ If you need a task done and your child hasn't done it, offer a choice:

> *Do you want to do it and earn the money, or would you rather I do it?"*

♦ No pressure. No nagging. Just a choice and its natural consequences.

♦ Imagine how much conflict this can eliminate between you and your child.

♦   Money and The Golden Rule:
>   *"He who has the gold makes the rules."*

♦   Whoever has earned the money gets to decide
how it is spent.
>   *For me to buy something with my money,*
>   *I have to believe it's a good value.*
>   *If you want to buy something with your*
>   *own money, you don't need my approval.*

♦   It's an especially valuable experience for a child
to work and save to buy a "big ticket" item.

♦ She will learn several things from this, all of which will be very useful to her in the long run:

> *Sometimes life involves trade-offs.*

> *Sometimes we have to choose between short-term wants and long-term goals.*

> *I can make these choices for myself.*

> *I am the one who controls the outcomes that I get in life.*

> *I can get something worthwhile if I am willing to work for it.*

♦ You will very shortly regret it if you succumb to what will be your child's natural and frequent request:

> *"Buy it for me now. Then I can pay you back."*

♦ If the child has already received the reward, there is no longer any motivation to work.

♦ He does not learn the connection between work and reward.

♦ The effort must come before the reward, or your child will not learn the connection.

♦ If you lend him money, he delays paying you back, and you end up nagging him to pay the debt.

♦ He learns two things from this, both of which are bad:

>   1. *I get what I want in life by badgering my mom.*
>   2. *My mom is a nag.*

♦   There will be an inevitable difference of opinion between parent and child as to what constitutes "necessity" versus "luxury".

♦   The parent gets to define what is necessity. If the child wants more than that, she can pay the difference with her own money.

♦   You set the limits, but give control to the child. Imagine how much conflict this can eliminate.

♦ Nothing is so effective for teaching a child what things cost as when he pays for them himself with money he has earned.

♦ He learns how many hours and how much effort it takes to earn that many dollars.

♦ Once your child has developed a work ethic and an ability to manage money, then you can indulge her some without spoiling her.

♦ If you start indulging her early on, she will come to expect it.

_____

♦ If you want to send a message to your child that education is important, consider paying him for excellent grades.

♦ Being a student is your child's current job.

♦ High pay for excellent performance is a realistic reflection of what he can expect to encounter later in life.

Surviving the Teenage Years

Surviving the Teenage Years

♦ From about the time your child enters 6th or 7th grade, your primary task as a parent is learning to "let go."

♦ From that time on, your child's behavior will become virtually unrecognizable.

♦ Beginning at about age 11 or 12, your previously lovely and loving child will begin to treat you as "the enemy" and will try to distance herself from you as much as possible—while still remaining frustratingly dependent on you.

♦ Bizarre behavior is not a sign you have failed as a parent or that your child is mentally ill.

♦ It simply means you are about to deal with the scourge of all parents: The dreaded teenager.

♦ Your teenager's behavior is fate's way of getting even with you for giving your own parents such a hard time.

♦ You don't fully appreciate your own parents until your kids become teenagers.

♦ All teenagers think their parents are hopelessly "out of it."

♦ All teenagers think their parents are embarrassingly weird.

♦ All teenagers find it humiliating to be seen in public with their parents.

♦ All teenagers would rather be orphans—except they need you to drive them to the mall.

- Every teenager believes he is the *only* one in the world whose parents are so hopelessly weird.

- Every parent wonders what in the world has gone wrong to produce such bizarre behavior and to deserve such total rejection.

♦ Do Not Take Anything Personally!!

♦ Bizarre behavior and total rejection are normal teenage behavior.

♦ The best way to deal with your teenager's incredibly low opinion of you is simply to acknowledge it.

♦ *"Yes, we are 'out of it.' Yes, we are weird. That's part of a parent's job description—to be hopelessly weird and 'out of it.'"*

---

*A Sense of Humor
May Be the Only Thing
That Will Get You Through
the Teenage Years.*

♦ You're dressed to go out, and your teenager says:

"You're not going to wear that, are you?"

Pick the Most Effective Response:

a.) What's wrong with the way I look?

b.) Why are you always so rude to me?

c.) Yes, I am wearing this. And I'm also going to hang a big sign around my neck that says: *"I'm Patti's Mom"* so the whole world will know you're related to this weird-looking person.

♦   The telephone is your teenager's link
    to the world. It is her means of
    maintaining contact with humanity.

♦   To forbid her to spend time on the
    phone is to make her feel isolated
    from her world.

♦ A teenager really *can* do homework while talking on the phone and watching television at the same time.

♦ Consider getting your teenager a separate telephone line—as a gift to yourself! It eliminates a lot of hassles.

♦ The fact that your teenager wants to sleep way past noon does not mean he is lazy and will never amount to anything. This is normal behavior.

♦ Mothers, do you remember when you were pregnant and you needed so much more sleep because of all the hormonal changes you were going through? This is how teenagers feel, all the time, for the same reason.

♦ It's not our place to tell others when to sleep or how much to sleep—as long as they produce the results they are responsible for.

♦ Focus on the results, not the methods.

♦ If you can simply accept your teenager's peculiar sleep habits as okay and not a problem, it will save you both a lot of aggravation.

♦   Did you hear about the teenager who lost 200 pounds in one day?

His dad got off his back.

♦   It's amazing what kids can do—if we will just stay out of their way.

♦ All teenagers have one primary mission in life:

> To establish their own identity, as separate and different from their parents as possible.

♦ They have no idea what that identity is supposed to be. It can be anything—as long as it's different from you.

♦   For adolescents and teenagers, dressing in a way that you see as outlandish is their way of establishing their own identity, their separateness from you, and their uniqueness as an individual.

♦   The fact that this "uniqueness" is totally defined by the fads and fashions of their peer group is not recognized by them as a contradiction.

♦ Don't take any of this personally. It's not an insult to you. It's a normal part of their development.

♦ If you allow your child some freedom in the way he dresses, he will feel less need to rebel in more serious ways.

♦ If you hate the way your teenager dresses, be grateful she doesn't have green hair and a ring in her nose.

♦ If she does have green hair and a ring in her nose, bite your tongue and consider this a character-building experience—your own!!

♦ Keep your mouth shut! The more you resist it, the longer she will cling to it. It will become a battle for control that you cannot win by force.

♦ Once you give up control willingly, she is then free to choose an appearance that is less bizarre.

♦ When your teenager's behavior seems deliberately designed to irritate you, it probably is.

♦ Take a deep breath, and repeat silently to yourself:

"This, too, shall pass."

♦ It *will* pass—and pretty quickly—as long as you don't make a major issue of it.

♦ There are two basic rules to life, which are essential in dealing with teenagers:

> 1.) Don't sweat the small stuff.
> 2.) It's all small stuff.

♦ Let the little irritations pass. Save your strength for the big issues. You'll need it.

♦   If your teenager can cause you to lose your cool, this gives him power over you. The angrier you get, the more powerful he feels.

♦   Your teenager's need to rebel is in direct proportion to your need to control.

♦ *"This is just a phase"* is very comforting to a parent, but a teenager finds it insulting. Repeat it to yourself as often as you need to, but don't say it out loud.

♦ Stay off your kid's back. If you're constantly nagging him about something, he will develop the habit of "tuning you out" and won't be listening when you do have something really important to say.

♦   If you want to offer advice to your teenager, consider this approach:

> *"I don't have all the right answers just because I'm the parent.*
>
> *You're just as smart as I am. The only advantage I have is experience because I'm older. I have more information about the likely outcomes of different courses of action.*
>
> *I'm going to share this information with you, and then you decide which course of action you think will work best for you."*

♦   If you can offer advice in the form of information rather than a command, your teenager can learn from it—and may even follow it willingly.

♦   If you try to impose it on him, he will feel the need to resist it.

♦   All parents are paranoid about whether their kids are using drugs. Here is the collective wisdom of the ages:

Symptoms of teenager who is using drugs:

>   *Withdrawn*   *Moody*
>   *Rebellious*   *Erratic behavior*

Characteristics of normal teenage behavior:

>   *Withdrawn*   *Moody*
>   *Rebellious*   *Erratic behavior*

♦ It's not fair to expect your child to achieve the things you always wanted to do, but never did.

♦ Not all children are cut out to be doctors or lawyers.

♦ Not all children want to be doctors or lawyers.

◆ You can't expect your child to live out *your* unfulfilled dreams.

◆ Support your child in following her own dreams.

◆ Isn't this what you wish your parents had done for you?

Separation Anxiety Revisited

The Light at the End of the Tunnel:
Separation Anxiety Revisited

♦ The ongoing aggravation and conflict between parents and teenagers serves a useful purpose:

> It's so unpleasant living together that it makes everyone ready for the kids to leave home.

♦ However, a strange thing may happen. Even though your rebellious teens can't wait to get away from your control—and at times you pray for them to be gone—it will be hard for you when the time finally does come.

- Don't worry if you have mixed feelings when it's time for your teenager to move out on his own.

- There is only one thing harder than watching your kids leave home:

    Watching them move back in.

♦ **Old Saying:**

> *If you allow your child to choose her own path, she will choose the one that leads back to you.*

♦ **Sobering Thought:**

> *You can measure your success as a parent by the way your child describes you to others.*

Dedication

To my parents, who gave me the foundation to build on and constant support along the way.

To my daughter, Patti, the greatest challenge and the greatest joy of my life.

Give The Gift of Successful Parenting
Mother's Day ✳ *Father's Day* ✳ *New Parents*
Prospective Parents ✳ *Parents of Teenagers*

Send me _____ copies of

SURVIVAL GUIDE FOR PARENTS: *How to Avoid Screwing Up Your Kids or Losing Your Own Sanity*

Name _____

Address _____

City _____

State _____ Zip _____

$9.95 per copy _____

TX residents add
$.80 per copy tax _____

Shipping cost: $3.00

For 2-Day Priority Mail,   Add $3.00 _____

TOTAL: _____

Phone _____

Send Check or money order to: Possibility Press, 6608 East Hill Drive, Austin, TX 78731

CHARGE CARD ORDERS, 24 hours, (512) 795-5006 or 1-800-460-6676. Fax (512) 795-5025

MC ( )   Visa ( ) # _____ Expires _____

Signature _____